Clinging to the Myth

Pádraig J. Daly

Clinging to the Myth

Pádraig J. Daly

First published in 2007 by
The Dedalus Press
13 Moyclare Road
Baldoyle
Dublin 13
Ireland

www.dedaluspress.com

ISBN 978 1 904556 58 9

Dedalus Press titles are represented in North America
by Syracuse University Press, Inc., 621 Skytop Road,
Suite 110, Syracuse, New York 13244, and in the UK by
Central Books, 99 Wallis Road, London E9 5LN

Printed and bound in the UK by Lightning Source,
6 Precedent Drive, Rooksley, Milton Keynes MK13 8PR, UK

Typesetting and design by Pat Boran
Cover image, Misty Morning © Martin Hendriks /iStockphoto

The Dedalus Press receives financial assistance from
An Chomhairle Ealaíon / The Arts Council, Ireland

In Memory of Mary Kirwan Daly,
My Mother

Contents

In Time of War

17.03.2003

What marvellous light
The sun on the trees throws!
The water carries a baulk of wood
As lightly as a brobh of straw,

Divebombing gulls drop from heaven
Onto the river,
Swans congregate
On a gold expanse beneath the reeds,

A metal bouy
Flashes messages to the sky,
Rooks pass,
Weary from their travail;

And all the while,
Planes move towards the desert;
And there is no knowing any longer
How long our day will last.

The Explosion at Windscale

Houses we stinted ourselves to buy,
Gardens carefully tended,
Fences dividing up our patches of permanence
Are all made useless.

The bread we eat poisons us,
We drink contamination from our taps,
Our hoarded wines
Are full-bodied and toxic.

Our rivermouths are blocked
To halt migrating smolt.
Our visitors move in awkward oversuits
Like travellers on the deserts of the moon.

The peoples of the world patrol our seas
So no unsuspecting stranger wanders near.

Cill Cais

after the Irish

Our woods cut down,
Nothing remaining but burnt stumps
And briars grown rank.

The woman absent,
The bell silent,
A chapel without mass.

No sound of goose
Or migrant duck,
No eagle hovering.

The honeybee
Has left its hive,
The cuckoo comes no more.

No hollyberries
Weigh a branch,
No trove of nuts.

Smutfall everywhere.
No noise of horse
Or bark of fox.

And still we pray
To Jesus,
Mary,

That she will home
To bonfires blazing,
Violins playing,
Circling dance.

Seán Ó Duibhir A' Ghleanna

after the Irish

Each morning then
I rose to sunlight,
Grunt of woodcock,
Bugle call;

Sound too
Of guns blazing,
Horses neighing,
Birds in flight;

A fox escaping,
A woman wailing
Above the carcasses
Of slaughtered geese.

But now the woods
Are felled about us,
Death's triumphant
On land and sky.

My dog is caged
Who once with leaping
Would stir the hearts
Of man and boy.

At night I sleep
By stream and river
And hide myself
In fern and whin,

Dreaming of flight
Across the ocean
And the silenced call
Of Seán Ó Duibhir.

Éamonn An Chnuic

after the Irish

What did he expect,
Tearing at my door,
Shouting with harsh voice,
Complaining that he was cold,
Hungry, in need of shelter:
That I would take
And hide him
Beneath my skirts?

He pleaded about how long
He had spent in snow and frost,
Having abandoned horse and plough
On the headland
Before ever he had sown the corn;
And there was no house anywhere
That would make him welcome:
He would have to wander now amid strangers.

He cajoled then
With talk of my eyes,
The curls in my hair;
And how he had loved none ever but me.
He would level hills for me
If I rode out with him:
We could admire fish and singing birds together
And listen to the deer moaning.

But the moan
Of guns firing in the valley
Was moan enough for me;
And the shouts of redcoats
Moving below us
On the roadway.

War

1.

Even as I walk,
Watching for sudden showers,
Where bluebells spread infinitely
Under trees,
I grow aware of an elsewhere,

Where a man,
Erect and stricken,
Walks out
To lift his lifeless daughter
From a roadway.

2.

A tern flies dispiritedly
To some nowhere on the water.
Swans lollop towards the shore.
Geese hiss at one another
With hostile intent.

Dunlins in gusts
Cheep over the bay.
Sea birds scream.
Our hearts in fleshy cages
Cry mercy.

3.

Here, where year on year
She listened for the call
Of the landrail,

There is nothing now
But the clatter of tanks
And the daily fluster around the dead.

Sin

for Gerard and Pauline Smyth

We sat in a circle before the house
Drinking bountiful wine.
Insects beat their wings,
Leaves in the forest rustled.

A girl began to sing
A sad song of greying love,
Somebody played a flute,
Someone began to dance.

As evening cast longer shadows,
A flock of birds
Rushed to the vines above the doorway,
Drowning out talk and laughter.

We threw coats over our shoulders,
Aware, even in our bliss,
That somewhere beyond us in the forest,
Hunters were slaying a huge and innocent bear.

Qoheleth

1.

Our short Summer is over.
Starlings have gathered and gone.
The brents return from their Northern day.

Winds blow across sands, pockmarked
By waterpools.
Wind vanishes.

Rain comes from the sea.
The sea fills, the sea ebbs:
Over and over.

2.

Perhaps
We pirouette

Under the stars,
Under the sun,

For a day,
For a year,

Frenetically,
Gravely;

And nothing then.

3.

Another city, the air cold.
We had rooms over the river.
All night long, we dreamt of boats
Toiling towards the enfolding ocean.

Toytown

In this toytown world we have created,
Even the few who come before You,
Come unbelievingly.

Among the others,
There is no hostility;
Only mystification

That there are those alive
Who cling still
To the Galilean myth,

Consider a God become flesh,
The word "God" itself
Describing unnecessary matter.

Fever

The God-fever
Burns itself out in us;

And though we glimpse Him still
Stir the lake,
Stride the clouds,

And point to Him and shout,
No one has any wish to hear.

Emptiness

All we have left
Is the manger and the straw
And the bundle of cloth on the floor
In a shabby room no one visits.

The child is gone;
And, to the kings who have come from afar,
All we offer is our emptiness.

Touch

We have never known miracles,
Yet believe that once in Galilee
God touched the world glancingly;

And nothing moved.
Yet all that saves us from despair
Resides there.

Roadway

A country road in Summer.
Suddenly, rows of cars
Skew-parked by fences.

Trees.
A church.
Hum of prayer.

A woman hurrying on dangerous heels,
A man settling his shirt,

Believing,
Wanting to believe.

Refuge

"Lord, You have been our refuge from one generation to the next."
—Psalm 90

In warm huddles
Around the tottering walls
Of ancient churches,
The overgrown graves
Of our ancestors:

Impassively,
They watch us
Take on opulence,
Forsake
The sheltering myth.

New Country

1.

The myth abandoned,
We walk by rivers
Where leaping salmon
No longer take our breath.

We go and come
In rooms, sealed
From the spectacular.

Water is poured,
Oil is spilled,
Bread is broken
In sweet nostalgia.

2.

One after another,
The faith-fetters are cast off.

Our freedom exhilirates us.
We dance *en plain air.*

And our children dance,
Wilder,

Wilder,
Wilder.

Burnets

What I hold onto now,
As high on the cliff
Papery burnets tremble,

Is that nothing—
No mouse or stone,
No human, blown

Like a smut
Across the vast array of things—
Is needless.

Eucharist

A circle of bread,
Broken,
Lifted up
In the full glare of sun.

Scatter of crumbs
Floating to the plate.

How easy
In green meadows
To credit
A myth of love.

Believers

You have led us out of the lovely houses of our
captivity,
Where we fed on fatted fowl
And sated ourselves on melons,

Into this desert,
Where winds, sand laden, sting our faces
And we walk blindly;

And we have no one
To touch the rock
And slake us with gushing water.

Cross

We pray and pray
And, though we surrender outcome
To the All-Beneficent,

We hope still,
Surreptitiously,
For tiny miracles;

And finish disappointed;
While down the mind's alleys
A frail figure

Points us
Towards the crossbeams
Of final failure.

Sadhbh

1.

I no longer count sheep
To bring on sleep.

I think of you,
Moving, speedy as a fish,
Across the floor,

Your cruel cast
Seeming buoyed on water,
Your mouth all slobber and laughter.

2.

If there were suffering we might accept
That would lessen yours,
We would grasp it eagerly.

We would lie before slaughtering swords,
Face bombs, walk
Into the path of Pershings,

Rather than stand before you
Without the words to explain
Why all our glory is crossed by grief.

Forgiveness

1.

The hardest thing
Is to offer forgiveness
Where forgiveness is inconsequential.

And you reach out merely
To lance your own
Suppurating soul.

2.

Caterpillars make themselves new
And fly,
Trees cover their wounds and thrive,
Skin sheds and mends
Septennially.

But what will repair
The unforgiven heart?

Queries

1.

From earliest days we were taught
That You are by us always to deliver us.

We drift about cheerily
In the bright light of such presumption

Until, from nowhere,
We are spun, face first, into mud.

Hobnails assail us,
The singing birds abandon our skies.

And are we to bide by You still?

2.

Are we, then,
The million sandhoppers
Along the sands,

Mayfly for their day
Over the lake,

Or the chestnut horse,
Ploughing an exultant path
Out into the waves?

3.

We know that You were in those rich fields
That climbed all over the spreading hills,

In the grey and tottering walls
That edged the roadway,

Even in the watery,
Intermittent sun.

But were You there too, all unrecognised,
In our faint and faltering hearts?

Postulant

She has come from everyday clamour
Into this calm.
She learns to lie down early,
To wake at dawn to laud her Maker,
To labour slowly at slow tasks.

She has been taught the names
Of all the cloths of the mass,
To speak trippingly of ambo,
Monstrance, catafalque,
To distinguish feast from feria.

Everything is measured and even,
The better to attend
To the susurrations of God.
Yet, even at prayer,
Her mind skelters elsewhere

Or fixes itself on ancient hurt,
Arguing, counterarguing,
Weeping inwardly;
And the One,
Glimpsed fleetingly before

In leaping fish or darting bird,
She finds now
In the squalor
Of her own
Unlovely heart.

Resurrection

There will be a day in the end
When there will be no need
To explain anything,

When we will row
Across the short channel
To the island

And find You standing
Where the white shingle
Drops steeply into sea,

Waiting to gather us
Under Your russet coat.

House: Mother at 80

The house becomes less ordered,
Dust is allowed to gather.

Her body sinks down into itself;
Her bones are brittle.

She is content to be quiet.
She has grown used to absences.

How long before she goes
Where we cannot follow to protect her?

According to Plotinus

It is no great thing
That mighty oaks should fall
Or candles flicker to a still;

Or that man,
Being mortal,
Should collapse.

Yet watching you begin
Your fitful spluttering-out,
Shatters my soft, unphilosophic heart.

Decision: Mother at 90

She reaches a thin hand
To clutch at mine:
She is frail and frightened.

She must leave all that years
Have made familiar
And go where she will lie at night

Listening to the moans of strangers.
No more dusting jugs and photographs,
Setting out cups,

Filling at evening her hot water jar,
Putting the door on double lock,
Climbing the short stairs to her bedroom.

If a clock ticks, it will not be hers.
If a phone rings in the night,
It will be for some other.

Leaving

She prays now,
With scarce hope,
That the Lord will take her

Before the day
When she must leave
All that the twists of life

Have made hers.
She has packed what she will need
Into two bags.

She has purchased a good skirt
And folded it neatly
In among the bedjackets and night attire.

She has gathered all her tablets
In a handbag,
With rosary, scissors, indigestion fluid.

We tell her
We can bring her back for visits.
She wonders if she will want to come.

Lunch

Today at lunch,
She asked me to set her fork
Onto her chicken,

Indistinguishable now
From the pale mound of potato mash.

She is disappointed with God
Who has left her in such confusion.

His Blindness

from the Irish of Tadhg Gaelach Ó Súilleabháin

My sorrow: my eyes, my sight, my vision, my face!
My defeat, my destruction, my melting, my woe,
My scalding of innards, my cry and my scream,
This scale that has fallen over my lovely globes!

Every cloud, every cover, every soft light haze
Lasts for a while and clears in time away
Except for these scales that will stay with me to the end,
Cutting my vision away from the shell of my head.

Oldcourt

Beyond the cemetery wall,
Three dowagers of the town
Are golfing.

It is a week before your death.
The trees are bone bare.
The ground squelches underfoot.

I go to where your father,
Mother, sister
Are buried.

I beg them
To preserve you
From madness and incapacity,

Little expecting
So cruel
And expeditious an answer.

The Call

When the call came, I was preparing for bed.
We had spent the afternoon together.
I can remember little of what we spoke about.
We laughed a lot.
Margaret arrived with fresh blouses.
You asked what you had ever done
To deserve your friends.
A girl brought in tea and soda bread.
We made plans for Sunday lunch.

Four hours had gone by.
Now they were wheeling you
Through the wide doors of a hospital,
Nurses flanking you with solicitude.
I anointed you quickly.
You retched emptily.
I held a bowl under your chin.
Your heart was racing.
You ordered me home to sleep.

I stayed,
Holding your hand.
Your breathing grew strained.
The nurses exited.
Gradually it came to me
That you were gone.

Afterwards they brought you to a small room.
You lay between white sheets
With candles beside you and a crucifix.

My brother and his wife
Were racing through the dark.
It would be hours before they were here.
I talked to you and talked until they came.

An Mhaighdean Mhara

Stealthily she went
From bunk to bunk,
Laying kisses

On the foreheads
Of her sleeping children,
Before leaving

To plunge, where she must,
Into the wondrous, starlit ocean,
Moving freely in the water

To encounter father, sister, friends,
All the seperated roisterers
Of her clan:

Your going too
Has left its stealthy mark
On our awaking brows.

Absence

1.

People tell me
They feel the dead
After they have died,
Helping, guiding,
In every predicament.

Since your death,
All I feel is sorrow;
And a gratitude
That you did not stay,
Bedbound or forgetful;

An absence also,
Everywhere:
Huge,
Profound
And unrelenting.

2.

I feel no need to pray for you,
Who lived your life entirely
In the shade of God;

Nor am I cheated
By the death of one
Grown awkward in the world.

What will chafe forever
Is the blank at my side
Where you were.

3.

I keep imagining you,
Emerging out of woodland,

Moving steadily on your stick,
Wearing the blue cardigan.

Between us,
There is an inlet of sea.

And I am rushing round to reach you;
And never do.

Greatgranddaughter

All day long
I have been full
Of news of her for you,
Forgetting over again
That you have died.

I wanted to tell you
How she loves football,
Can do jigsaws
Almost in her sleep,
Is frightened of dogs.

Dolls bore her,
Even those that cry
Realistic tears;
But she loves to slop
In her play kitchen.

I wanted to describe
The long curls
That fall coquettishly
Onto her forehead,
The quick flick

That sweeps them back;
To tell you too
How her smile
Lights the countryside
As once did yours.

End of the Road

You were always at the end of the road,
Eager for the trivia of my journey:

Fog along the Comeraghs,
Vintage tractors holding the traffic back,

Speedchecks in Leamybrien,
The laying of pipes;

And another funeral in the town:
Young men in suits, women sombre,

Busyness about the hearse,
The shuffle of mourners to the grave,

Some other family grieving.

Death

She has gone out alone
Into the realm of stars.

Do not let her be lost
In the windy deserts
Of the universe.

Do not let her journey
Be a frightened one.

Let there be arms at last
To pull her home.

On Her Birthday

Let her have a warm sun in the sky.
Next, a small expanse of water;
And water moving over stones.
Then, hills all around,
Ridged with hawthorn fences.

Provide a house for her,
Set amid privet and roses,
In a yard enclosed by stone buildings.

Let her have a chair in the shade,
Where she can finger her beads,
Half hearing the coughing of calves,
The hens' complaining,
Noise of children in the haggard.

Tears

1.

Do other people,
Driving long journeys through the countryside,
Sitting privately in their rooms,
Months after a death,
Fall too to sudden weeping,

As if the loved one had left
Only moments before
And there was no love anymore
In the world?

2.

Tears don't come
At proper hours and intervals

But, suddenly,
In the flow of talk,

Waiting in a queue,
Calming a neglected dog.

Awe

Make a roadway along the hill
And climb it on your knees
To where the old are gathered,
Feebly awaiting death,

Some timorous,
Some confused,
Some serenely watching
The changing colours of the valley.

Approach them with awe.
Notice their laved skin,
Their sweet-smelling hair.
Bow before them and give praise.

Rivertown

1.

Before the settlers moved their town
Out here nearer the river,
This was a copse of songbirds.

I hear them still,
Early at morning,
Announcing the end of dark,

Laying out prior claim
To their small tranches
Of territory.

2.

The rain throws itself heavily
Upon wet expanses of river
And, drop by drop,
Loses itself in vastness.

Lights fall icily on the water,
Inconsequent defences
Against the naught
Of the universe.

Gulls shriek,
Pulling at raw meat
Beneath the feet of by-passers.
Their yellow beaks are edged with blood.

3.

Soon my boat will come
And take me beyond lights and harbour
And people walking casually to pubs,

Out to where all is cold,
All is silent,
All is nothing and dark.

4.

The party is over.
We step into the rain
And are stopped still

By the amber lamps
Of the town below us
And dark light on water.

5

All day long, good people in boats
Go up and down a square of river,
Dragging hooks along its bed,
Searching for his lean young body.

His family stare into the cold
Unresponsive water.
His friends weep:

And I have no prayer left
To pray with them.

6.

Six roses in a vase,
White linen,
Unlit candles.

Glass coloured to show
Rope, pulleys,
The movement of sailboats.

A bird climbing,
A bird alighting,
Brushing the window with shadow.

Long Days of Summer

1.

The wonder is that there aren't ghosts
And that those walkers along Maoil a' Chóirne,
On childhood Summer days

When dog daisies swept in abundant swathes
Through the verge,
Inhabit there no longer.

2.

Midsummer:
And we are above the sea
In flowerstudded meadows,
Talking easily,
Sucking the sweetness
From wisps of grass.

In my heart
I am captured
By your symmetries,
Longing to build tabernacles
As if all this that you are
Were distilled from your own plenty.

3.

At every gap,
Sparrows lift from their games in the dust.

Farm-reared pheasants race in confusion
Across the path of oncoming trucks.

Someone young has died in one of the towns:
A vast silence holds the mourners.

Trees hem the roadway,
As sensuous day prolongs itself.

4.

Near the close of evening,
We are meandering towards the river,
Faces red from wine and sunshine.

Two dogs run before us.
Barley darkens a rising field.
God is surely in the whistling of our hearts.

Chestnuts

Under the gigantic boughs,
Three small boys gather chestnuts,

Each thrilled by the brown miracle
Beneath unwelcoming husks,

Each collecting his own hoard,
Dreaming of conkerbattles ahead,

But distracted for a moment
By the neonate beauty in his hands.

Gift

Because she was beautiful,
He willed her virtuous
And offered her, recklessly,
His permeable heart.

Jetty

The little jetty
Ran out at an angle
Below the bridge.

The spring tides
Climbed granite walls
To within inches of its crown.

Towards night, the boy,
Forgetting cautions,
Stepped out along its length

To stand,
Each pore intent,
Level with the threatening depths.

Lore

There was a tribe in that place,
Whose savants strapped a tiny bird
To the breasts of all their corpses;

Perhaps to startle their hearts to life again,
Perhaps to sing them
Into the fields of death.

Sometimes still we tread on sward,
Where deep under earth
Small birds stir their clay-encumbered wings.

Alzheimers

for Frank

Seeing you as you are
Unnerves me,
All that you were
Evaporated.

Where does your mind wander now?
Does it wake ever,
Welcoming us to the door
Of that ramshackle house in Inchicore,

Leading us through the hall,
Urging us to watch the step,
Opening the whiskey with a twist,
Calling down to your wife in the kitchen?

And how do you remember her?
Her mirth? Her tenderness? Her thousand vendettas?
Will we never again listen
To you chuckle through your yarns—

The girl in your bedroom in France,
Making your boss gasp at your worldliness?
The friend from Cork
Reinventing himself with Trinity intonation?

How does the blank that keeps your features link
With the glory that was you?

Funeral

I could have spared myself the journey:
Wintery sunlight,
Roads dangerous with ice,
My presence of no consequence to the mourners.

But I was mourning too,
For you and for her;
And being here
Was all I had left to do forever.

A Father

He never understood parks—
Laying vast acreage aside
And hiring men to mow and trim the grass
When cattle and sheep might graze it happily.

He could not comprehend travel
When you had the Comeraghs to one side,
The sea to the other
And the wonders of the street at your door.

He abhorred debt, approved of strikes,
Loved Irish, distrusted republicans.
He rejoiced in fields brassy with cabbage,
In new roads through stubborn hillsides.

He cherished ways by the tide,
Boats in the ocean, cards at night,
The hush around a song,
The braonín before bed.

Grandmother

The old people spoke of her young beauty.
My mother remembered her as full of prayers and *piseogs*,   ˅
With a tight hold on the purse.

When the men were in the fields,
She would take down her tin moneybox
To iron the wrinkles from the notes.

(The family were afraid
She would go soft on her deathbed
And hand all to an avaricious priest).

I remember her dark hair,
Pinned in a circle around her face,
Her long black aprons,

I remember the brass candlesticks when they waked her,
The white sheets,
The woman who came with a huge bag to lay her out;

The grief breaking over my father in the graveyard.

Jimmy

He was one never spoken of: the eldest son,
Buried before we were born in the County Asylum.

When my father took the bus to visit him,
He would greedily grab fags and fruit,
Then sit without talking.

Years later we heard of his obsession with a beautiful child,
How the guards were sent for to take him from harm;
Stories too of how he was handsome and loved dancing.

Now all those we might ask about him are dead.

Slivers

Her day went by
In farmyard drudgery,
Keeping house,
Tending child and animals.

At evening,
And even into dark,
She would go among her flowers,
Watering carefully,

Carrying slivers of moon
In her bucket.

Úna

We drove to the sandy edges of land.
I recall the powdery gold of the dunes,
Screeching birds;
Your beauty, a reed in the tide.

We eat in a pub in the fields.
You took sodabread and tea.
I had potato and fish.

You had come for refuge.
Your trusted props were gone.
Your lover, Christ,
Was blasting you white.

Later,
In a thin wind,
We walked the shore.
The sun poured benediction on the water.

Missionary

in memory of Kevin Cullen

After years of dust
And exuberant disarray,
He comes again to his own country,

To bleak skies,
Empty worshipping places
And a people flocking to a golden calf.

Bauchi

At the set hours of prayer,
The men put business aside,
Don gleaming robes
And converge from a thousand pathways
To acclaim the One.

Rickety lorries, carrying the slogans
Of Flemish coalimporters,
Spanish fruitmerchants
Slow down to give them way.
Children drag carts on tin-lid wheels.
They wear flip-flops cut from tyres.

In the hotel, faded drapes hold back the sun.
The guests are mostly Arab.
The women, swathed in black,
Reveal gold-braceleted arms,
Heavily jeweled fingers.
There is no drink to be had
For thirsty Christians.
The plumbing is in total collapse.

Petrol is for sale by the roadside
At black-market prices.
There is dust everywhere
As hens and goats and every living thing
Celebrate the great cacophony.

Sabon Gida Kanar

The Fulani move their cattle
Onto the grassy ground
Beside the trees.

Women approach from the village
To buy milk.

The beasts settle complacently
As if this, at last, were a place
With no going onward.

Printed in the United States
75491LV00002B/5